Finance Glow - Your Path to Financial Empowerment

Essential Financial Literacy for Everyone

Copyright Information

© 2024 Leasia Ezeogu. All rights reserved.

First edition, published 2024.

ISBN: 9798334035997

All Rights Reserved
No part of this book may be reproduced, distributed, or transmitted in any form or by any means, including photocopying, recording, or other electronic or mechanical methods, without the prior written permission of the publisher, except in the case of brief quotations embodied in critical reviews and certain other noncommercial uses permitted by copyright law.

Disclaimer
This book is for informational purposes only. The author assumes no responsibility for errors or omissions, or for damages that may result from the use of the information contained herein. The advice and strategies contained herein may not be suitable for every situation. It is recommended to consult with a professional where appropriate.

Table of Contents

Introduction

Did you know that nearly 40% of Americans wouldn't be able to cover an unexpected $400 expense without selling something or borrowing money? Or that 25% of adults have no savings at all for emergencies? These statistics might sound alarming, but they underscore a crucial reality - financial literacy is not a luxury—it's a necessity. It's these kinds of gaps in financial knowledge that "Finance Glow" aims to bridge.

I'm Leasia Ezeogu, and my mission is to empower you with financial knowledge that will transform your life. Like many of you, I navigated the treacherous waters of financial uncertainty. Having experienced financial challenges and uncertainty firsthand, I was inspired to pursue a career in accounting. Today, I am grateful to have the opportunity to give back by educating and empowering others.

My quest for stability led me to pursue an accounting degree, through which I unearthed invaluable lessons. It's these lessons on budgeting, saving, investing, and more that I'm excited to share with you in this book.

In this guide, we'll uncover the basics of budgeting, the importance of saving, and the often-intimidating world of investing. We'll demystify credit scores and discuss how to invest smartly. This book gives you not just the information, but the confidence to take control of your financial destiny.

On this path, you might wonder what makes this book different from others. It's the approach—clear, concise, and conversational. Financial jargon can be intimidating, but here, we'll break it down into bite-sized, digestible pieces. Picture this - understanding finances will soon feel as natural as planning a weekend outing.

I'll use real-life examples and specific numbers to make abstract concepts tangible. For instance, think of budgeting like organizing a bookshelf. Each category of expense is a shelf, and you have only so much space. By ensuring that the essentials—like rent and groceries—are within reach and organized, you'll stop things from tumbling down.

Remember, financial literacy isn't about being perfect with money; it's about being informed and making better choices.

So, let's dive in and start this journey together. Your path to financial empowerment begins now.

Chapter 1 - Understanding Financial Basics

Have you ever tried to assemble a complex piece of furniture without the instructions? It's trying to decode without understanding the language, getting more confused with each step. Understanding financial basics feels similar; it can be overwhelming and muddling without a clear, straightforward guide. But here's the good news - financial literacy is your instruction manual for life's financial furniture.

Financial literacy is the foundation of your financial journey. It's not just about balancing your checkbook or knowing the difference between a savings account and an investment account, although those are crucial elements. Financial literacy equips you with the skills to create a budget and stick to it, save effectively, invest wisely, and manage debt. You become adept at making informed decisions that lead to financial stability and independence.

The Psychology of Finance

Understanding the basics of finance is essential, but grasping the psychological aspect is equally crucial. Let's say you have the perfect budget, you save diligently, and you're well-versed in investment strategies. Yet, despite all this, you find yourself triggered by an unexpected sale or emotional spending. Why does this happen? The answer lies in the complex interplay between our emotions and our money habits.

Emotional Spending is a classic example. Many people, after a tough day, find solace in retail therapy. A beautiful dress or the latest gadget becomes a temporary escape, but this fleeting happiness often results in financial regret. What's happening here is a release of dopamine, a neurotransmitter linked to pleasure and reward. It feels great in the moment, but can lead to poor financial health if uncontrolled. Recognizing this can help you develop healthier coping mechanisms, such as allocating a small amount for guilt-free spending, while keeping your main finances intact.

Scarcity Mindset is another psychological hurdle. Have you ever held onto money too tightly, fearing it will run out? This mindset often stems from past experiences of financial instability or cultural teachings. For example, someone who grew up in a household where money was always tight may view finances through a lens of scarcity. They might save excessively but avoid investing due to the fear of loss. By understanding this, you can start shifting towards an *abundance mindset*. This involves acknowledging your financial fears but making calculated decisions that allow for growth and not just hoarding of resources.

Consider Jake, a recent college graduate. He landed a well-paying job but was overwhelmed by the freedom to spend. Without financial discipline, his love for new tech gadgets saw his credit card debt skyrocket. Knowing this, he decided to implement a **Reward System** for budgeting. He set aside a specific amount each month for discretionary spending. This way, he indulged in his interests but stayed within limits. Over time, this helped him stay on track while satisfying his desire for the latest gear.

Behavioral economists explain these patterns using theories like Prospect Theory, which shows that people feel the pain of loss more intensely than the pleasure of gain. This can lead to irrational financial decisions, such as holding onto failing investments due to the fear of realizing a loss. Understanding these psychological nuances can help you make more rational decisions, like cutting losses when necessary and thinking long-term.

By being aware of the emotional currents influencing your financial choices, you can navigate your way to better financial health. It's about creating a balanced strategy that considers both your psychological triggers and your financial goals. Remember, the goal is to empower yourself to not only understand money but also to understand the factors that influence your decisions about money. This dual awareness can guide more informed and disciplined financial actions.

Key Terms Explained

Let's explore the essential terms that will form the bedrock of your financial literacy journey. Understanding these concepts is a game-changer. They will empower you to make smart financial decisions and take control of your financial future. So, let's dive right in.

Budgeting - Budgeting is like creating a roadmap for your money. Without it, it's easy to lose track and end up in a financial mess. A budget is a plan that shows how much money you receive (your income) and how much money you spend (your expenses). It sounds simple, but it can change your life. By budgeting, you see where your money goes, make adjustments, and set financial goals.

For example, let's look at Sarah. She earns $3,000 a month. She used to spend $200 on dining out and $150 on subscriptions she didn't really use. By creating a budget, she realized this and cut back those expenses. Now, that $350 goes into her savings account.

Saving - Saving is the act of setting aside money for future use. This can be for emergencies, big purchases, or retirement. Savings give you security and peace of mind, knowing you're prepared for unexpected expenses. A good rule of thumb is to save at least **20%** of your income each month.

Everyone's financial situation is unique, so there's no one-size-fits-all approach to saving. It's essential to find a balance between saving and spending that works for you. That said, the earlier you start saving, the better. This allows for more significant growth over time.

Investing - Investing is using your money to make more money. Unlike saving, which just keeps your money safe, investing aims to grow your wealth. This can be through stocks, bonds, real estate, or other vehicles. Investing comes with risks, but it also offers the potential for higher returns.

The average inflation rate is around **2-3%** per year. If your savings account only earns **0.5%** interest, you're losing money in the long run. Investing can help combat inflation and build wealth over time.

Credit Scores - Your credit score is like a report card of your financial responsibility. It's a numerical expression of your creditworthiness, ranging from **300 to 850**. A high score means you're a low-risk borrower, which can help you get better interest rates on loans and credit cards. Your credit score is influenced by your payment history, credit utilization, length of credit history, and types of credit.

Think about it this way - if you're a landlord, would you rather rent your property to someone with a history of paying rent on time or someone who frequently misses payments? That's what lenders see when they look at your credit score.

Understanding and mastering these key terms is your step towards financial empowerment. You aren't just learning definitions but acquiring tools that will help you navigate the financial world with confidence and ease. Each dollar you save, invest, or manage wisely brings you closer to financial independence.

Chapter 2 - Creating a Budget

Now picture this - you're an artist about to start a masterpiece. Without a clear plan, your painting might become a jumbled mess of colors and shapes. Creating a budget works the same way. It's your blueprint for financial success. It guides every stroke of your financial decisions and ensures the end result is something you're proud of. Without a budget, managing money can feel like fumbling in the dark.

A budget is much more than just a list of numbers. It's a detailed map that helps you navigate the twists and turns of your financial journey. It identifies where every penny you earn should go, ensuring you make the most of your income. Remember *Sarah* from the last chapter? Budgeting is what helped her transform her paycheck-to-paycheck lifestyle into one of financial stability and growth.

Think of budgeting as giving each dollar a job. Every dollar should know its purpose, whether it's paying for necessities, saving for the future, or being set aside for investments. This approach removes the uncertainty and prevents money from slipping through your fingers unnoticed.

Steps to Create a Budget

Creating a budget might sound intimidating, but it's simpler than you think. It's about developing a plan for your money, ensuring you know where every single dollar goes. Let's break it down into straightforward steps that anyone can follow.

Track Income and Expenses

Start by writing down all your sources of income. This could include your salary, side gigs, freelance work, or any other money coming in. Next, list every expense. Yes, every coffee, subscription, and grocery bill. Details matter here. The goal is to get a clear picture of your financial life.

Let's say you earn $3,000 a month and spend $2,500 on rent, groceries, utilities, and other expenses. Knowing this information is the first step to taking control of your finances.

Categorize Expenses

Once you have all your income and expenses listed, categorize them. Split them into essentials like rent, utilities, and food, and non-essentials like entertainment and dining out. This helps you understand which expenses are necessary and which can be trimmed.

For the above $2,500 example, let's say $1,500 is spent on essential expenses and $1,000 on non-essentials. The essential category could be further broken down into fixed expenses like rent and variable expenses like groceries. The non-essential category could be divided into discretionary expenses like dining out and other subscriptions.

Set Financial Goals

Define what you want to achieve with your money. This could be paying off debt, saving for a vacation, or building an emergency fund. Let's say you want to save $500 a month for an emergency fund. This goal will guide your budgeting decisions, ensuring you allocate enough money towards it each month.

Allocate Funds - Choosing Your Budgeting System

Now that you have tracked your income and expenses, categorized them, and set financial goals, it's time to allocate your funds. This is where the magic happens—where your plan turns into action. Let's explore three popular budgeting systems and find the one that works best for you.

The 50/30/20 Rule

The 50/30/20 rule is a straightforward budgeting method that divides your after-tax income into three main categories -

1. **50% for Needs** - These are essential expenses such as rent, utilities, groceries, transportation, health insurance, and minimum debt payments.
2. **30% for Wants** - These are discretionary expenses like dining out, entertainment, vacations and other non-essential purchases.
3. **20% for Savings and Debt Repayment** - This portion goes towards saving for emergencies, retirement, or paying down debt. If you don't yet have an emergency fun, consider prioritizing this first.

Let's say you earn $4,000 a month after taxes. Using the 50/30/20 rule, you allocate $2,000 for needs, $1,200 for wants, and $800 for savings and debt repayment. This simple structure helps you make sure your priorities are covered while still enjoying your life.

Zero-Based Budgeting

Zero-based budgeting gives every dollar a job. The goal is to have your income minus expenses equal zero. This method requires detailed planning and ongoing tracking to ensure every dollar is accounted for.

Example -

Income of $6,300 per month.

- Rent - $2,100
- Utilities - $400
- Groceries - $500
- Transportation - $200
- Childcare - $1,000
- Dining Out - $300
- Entertainment - $200
- Savings - $700
- Debt Repayment - $600
- Miscellaneous: $300

Total - $6,300

This way, every dollar is allocated towards a specific expense or financial goal, leaving no room for unplanned spending.

Envelope System

The envelope system is a cash-based budgeting method. You divide your cash into envelopes

labeled with different spending categories.
When the money in an envelope is gone, you
stop spending in that category.

Example - Let's take a working woman who uses
the envelope system and allocates her $5,000
monthly income into various envelopes -

- Rent - $1,800
- Utilities - $250
- Groceries - $450
- Transportation - $300
- Childcare: $800
- Fun Money - $300
- Savings - $700
- Debt Repayment - $400

She withdraws $5,000 in cash at the beginning
of the month and distributes it into her
envelopes. This tactile method helps her stay
disciplined and avoid overspending.

Finding Your Best Fit

Choosing the right budgeting system depends
on your financial habits and personality. The
50/30/20 rule is excellent for those seeking
simplicity. Zero-based budgeting suits detail-
oriented individuals who enjoy tracking every
penny. The envelope system is perfect for

people who need strict control over their spending.

Tip - You can even combine elements from different systems. For example, use the 50/30/20 rule for an initial allocation, then apply zero-based principles to fine-tune your plan.

Remember, the aim is not to restrict you but to empower you to make informed financial decisions. Budgeting is about knowing where your money goes and making it work towards your goals. Each system is a tool—pick the one that makes your financial life clear and manageable.

Tools and Resources

Creating and sticking to a budget can seem like a daunting task. Luckily, in our digital age, there's an abundance of tools designed to make managing your finances seamless and straightforward. Let's dive into some resources that can help you take control of your money with ease.

1. Rocket Money

Rocket Money is a fantastic app for anyone looking to cut out unnecessary subscriptions and bills. Imagine you're trying to trim the fat off your budget - Rocket Money acts like a magnifying glass, showing you all those sneaky subscriptions that siphon your cash. It alerts you to forgotten subscriptions and even helps you cancel them right from the app. You'd be surprised how quickly those $5, $10, or even $20 monthly charges add up!

2. Mint

Mint is a powerhouse for tracking spending, and it's totally free. Think of Mint as your personal financial assistant. It categorizes your purchases, tracks your expenses, and even alerts you when you're nearing your budget limits. By providing a clear picture of your spending habits, Mint can help you make informed decisions and stay within your budget.

3. YNAB (You Need a Budget)

YNAB operates on the principle that every dollar should have a job. It's perfect for proactive management. YNAB helps you break the paycheck-to-paycheck cycle by encouraging you to live on last month's income. The app's dynamic nature means you're always making real-time adjustments to your budget based on your spending.

YNAB leverages the psychological concept of "loss aversion." By making you allocate every dollar, you become more conscious of your spending, reducing the likelihood of wasteful expenses.

4. Every Dollar

Every Dollar is a zero-based budgeting tool created by financial guru Dave Ramsey. It's simple and user-friendly, making it an excellent choice for those new to budgeting. You start by giving every dollar a purpose, ensuring your income minus expenses equals zero. This method forces you to account for every penny, reducing frivolous spending.

Once you get the hang of budgeting, you might not need the digital assistance. A simple pen and paper can be all you need to stay on top of your finances. The important thing is finding a system that works for you and sticking with it.

Chapter 3 - Saving Strategies

Imagine you're setting out on a long-awaited vacation. You wouldn't just grab your suitcase, head to the airport, and hope for the best. Planning your savings should be approached the same way. It's all about preparation, knowing your destination, and mapping out your best route to get there.

Saving strategies are the hidden engines behind financial empowerment. They propel you towards your goals, be it buying a home, starting a business, or simply having an emergency fund. Yet, saving money isn't just about stashing away cash in a jar or under a mattress. It's about being intentional and strategic, making your money work for you in ways you might not have imagined before.

To drive this point home, consider a study by the American Psychological Association, which found that people with clear financial goals and savings plans report lower levels of stress and higher overall well-being. It's psychological really; knowing you have a financial cushion brings immense peace of mind.

Numbers don't lie. If you save $200 a month, in five years you will have $12,000, not accounting for any interest you might earn. Break that down - that's cutting a few takeouts or coffee runs. Simple steps like these pave the way for more significant financial security and freedom.

The key is to be proactive, not reactive. Waiting until you're in a financial crisis to start saving is like repairing a roof during a rainstorm. The leaks could have been prevented with prior careful planning and consistent effort. Instead, begin now, even if it's with small, manageable amounts.

In this chapter, we'll explore various saving strategies tailored to different lifestyles and goals. Whether you're a student, a working professional, or nearing retirement, we'll cover approaches that fit your situation.

Building an Emergency Fund - Your Financial Lifeline

Imagine standing on a tightrope without a safety net. It's risky and stressful, right? That's what living without an emergency fund feels like for many people. An emergency fund is that safety net, ready to catch you when life throws

surprises your way. It's not just about money –
it's about peace of mind and financial security.

First things first, start with a clear goal. Aim to
save at least **3-6 months' worth of living
expenses**. This includes rent or mortgage,
utilities, groceries, transportation, and other
essential costs. If your monthly expenses are
$3,000, your target should be between $9,000
and $18,000. This might sound daunting, but
breaking it down makes it achievable.

Set aside a specific amount each month. Even if
it's just $50 or $100 initially, consistency is key.
For example, **saving $100 a month will give
you $1,200 in a year.** Not bad, right? You can
always increase the amount as your financial
situation improves.

Choose a separate, easily accessible account for
your emergency fund. High-yield savings
accounts are a good option. They offer higher
interest rates than regular savings accounts,
helping your money grow while still being
readily available. Remember, the goal is not just
to save but to have quick access to funds when
needed. There are countless stories of how
emergency funds have provided a lifeline.
Consider Jane, who lost her job unexpectedly.
Her $10,000 emergency fund covered her living
expenses for five months. This allowed her to

focus on finding a new job without the panic of financial instability. It wasn't just money; it was a buffer that gave her the confidence and security to navigate a tough time.

The key to building an emergency fund is to start now. Don't wait for the perfect moment. Begin with small steps, be consistent, and watch your fund grow. Your future self will thank you.

Effective Saving Techniques

Building an emergency fund is just one piece of the puzzle. To truly take control of your finances, you need a robust saving strategy. Let's dive into some effective techniques that can make a huge difference without overwhelming you.

Automating your savings is like setting your financial goals on autopilot. Think of it as a stealthy way to save money without even noticing. Here's how it works - Schedule automatic transfers from your checking account to your savings account each month. Set a specific date, ideally aligned with payday. Start small if you need to—$50 or $100 can be a great start. The key is consistency. Over time, these small amounts add up.

For instance, let's say you set up an automatic transfer of $100 a month. By the end of the year, you'll have $1,200 saved up effortlessly. If you start with $200, you'll have $2,400. That's the beauty of automation—it removes the temptation to spend, ensuring your savings goal is consistently met.

High-Yield Savings Accounts - Maximizing Your Returns

Don't let your money sit idly. A high-yield savings account offers higher interest rates than traditional savings accounts. This means your money works harder for you, even when it's just sitting in the bank. Imagine having $5,000 in a regular savings account earning 0.01% interest. That's a mere 50 cents a year! Now, put that same amount in a high-yield savings account with a 5% interest rate. You'd earn $250 annually. Big difference, right?

Choose an account that aligns with your needs. Online banks often offer better rates than traditional brick-and-mortar banks. They also provide easy access, often without minimum balance requirements. Look for accounts with **no monthly fees** to ensure you're not losing money unnecessarily.

Some of the best high-yield savings accounts include Wealth front, American Express, Ally Bank, Marcus by Goldman Sachs, and Discover Savings. Do your research and compare rates to find the best fit for you.

Certificates of Deposit (CDs) - Safe and Steady

If you're looking for a safe place to park your money and earn more interest than a savings account, consider a Certificate of Deposit (CD). CDs have fixed interest rates, which means your money grows at a predictable rate. It's like locking your money in a safe and watching it grow. Just be mindful of the term length – you won't be able to access your funds without a penalty until the CD matures.

For example, if you invest $5,000 in a 1-year CD with a 4% interest rate, by the end of the year, you'll have $5,200. That's $200 for essentially doing nothing. CDs can get a bit more complicated with different terms and interest rates, so do your research before investing. The goal at the end of the day is to have a strong financial cushion for any unexpected expenses. These saving techniques and resources are just some of the many ways to help you achieve that goal. *It's never too late to start!*

Chapter 4 - Investing 101

Investing is essentially putting your money to work for you. It's about making your money grow over time, much like how a well-tended garden flourishes. **Why should you invest?** The value of money changes over time due to inflation. Keeping your money in a standard savings account means it's likely losing value over time.

On the other hand, investing helps counteract inflation and increases your wealth. For example, if you invest $1,000 in an index fund with an average annual return of 7%, your money could grow to around $7,612 in thirty years. Isn't that amazing?

We're not talking about Wall Street tycoons; everyday people like you and I invest successfully all the time. Remember, the goal here is to make your money work for you. Your investments could fund your retirement, help buy your dream home, or ensure your children's education. However, it's important to understand that investing comes with risks. Knowing these risks and how to manage them is critical.

Simplicity is key when starting. You don't need to master every term or trend. Terms like "stocks," "bonds," and "mutual funds" might seem intimidating. But once you break them down, they're quite straightforward. Stocks, for instance, are parts of a company that you can own. When the company does well, so do you. Bonds are loans you give to businesses or governments that pay you back with interest. Mutual funds pool money from lots of people to invest in a diversified assortment of stocks or bonds. Each type has its pros and cons, and the more you know, the better choices you can make.

Here's where *psychology* plays a role. Studies show that people who have a sound investment plan are less stressed and more optimistic about their future. It's all about feeling secure, and knowing you have a plan provides that. Start thinking of your investment strategy as a long-term journey rather than a get-rich-quick scheme. This will help manage expectations and provide the mental cushion to stay the course during market ups and downs.

Understanding Different Investment Options

So, you're ready to dive into the world of investing. Congratulations! Let's break down the types of investments you should know about. We'll focus on three primary categories - stocks, bonds, and mutual funds. Each offers unique benefits and risks, so understanding them is crucial.

Stocks - Owning a Piece of the Pie

Imagine you love a particular tech company, and you want in on its success. By purchasing stocks, you're buying a small slice of that company. When the company makes a profit, so do you through dividends and capital gains. Stocks often provide higher returns than other investments.

For example, if you bought $1,000 worth of Amazon stock in 2000, it would be worth over $1.6 million today. However, such returns are rare and represent an exceptional case. Stocks can be volatile, and their value can fluctuate widely depending on market conditions. It's essential to be emotionally prepared for this rollercoaster ride.

To start investing in stocks, you can purchase individual company stocks or invest in a stock market index fund, which tracks the performance of a specific group of stocks. Platforms like Fidelity, Vanguard, Robinhood, E-Trade, and TD Ameritrade make it easy to buy and sell stocks online.

VOO - Your Ticket to the S&P 500

Think of VOO as a way to own a piece of the 500 biggest companies in the U.S. without having to pick individual stocks. VOO is an exchange-traded fund (ETF), which means it pools money from many investors to buy shares of all these large companies that make up the S&P 500 Index. This gives you broad exposure to the U.S. stock market.

Investing in VOO is like getting a slice of a massive pie, where the pie represents the performance of top companies like Apple, Microsoft, and Amazon. It's known for having low fees, making it a smart choice for those looking to invest without breaking the bank.

For example, if you invested in VOO over time, you could see your investment grow as these companies succeed and the market rises. Plus, because you're investing in many companies at once, you're spreading out your risk, which is great for beginners who might be nervous about picking stocks.

Getting started with VOO is easy! You can buy shares through online brokerages like Fidelity, Vanguard, Robinhood or E-Trade, just like you would with individual stocks. This simplifies the investing process and helps you build a diversified portfolio without too much hassle.

Fidelity 500 Index Fund (FXAIX) - Investing Made Simple

The Fidelity 500 Index Fund (FXAIX) can be thought of as a large pie that includes slices from the top 500 companies in the U.S. This mutual fund offers a fantastic opportunity for investors who want exposure to a diverse range of successful businesses without the hassle of selecting individual stocks. By investing in FXAIX, you're not just betting on a single company; you're sharing in the performance of 500 of the most prominent firms, which effectively spreads out your risk.

One of the standout features of FXAIX is its low expense ratio, meaning more of your investment capital remains in the market, which can lead to potentially higher returns over time. This makes FXAIX especially appealing for beginners looking for a straightforward way to enter the stock market while benefiting from diversification and professional management.

Additionally, FXAIX tracks the performance of the S&P 500, which historically has provided solid long-term growth, making it a reliable choice for building wealth. The fund also reinvests dividends, allowing your investment to grow even faster. Overall, FXAIX represents a smart, cost-effective strategy to invest in the stock market and grow your money over time.

Bonds - The Safer Loan Option

Bonds are like lending money to a company or government. In return, they pay you interest over a fixed period. Think of it as helping a friend start a business, and they agree to pay you back with interest. Bonds are generally considered safer than stocks because you know what interest you'll earn and when you'll get your money back.

However, they usually offer lower returns. A good example is U.S. Treasury Bonds. They are almost risk-free and provide a steady income stream. Yet, because they are safer, the returns are modest. Investing $10,000 in a 10-year Treasury Bond at a 3.5% annual interest rate will yield a total of $3,500 in interest by maturity.

Mutual Funds - Diversification Made Easy

Mutual funds pool money from many investors to buy a diversified portfolio of stocks, bonds, or other securities. It's like joining a community garden, where everyone contributes, and everyone benefits from the harvest. This spreading of risk means that if one investment within the fund performs poorly, others might do well, balancing the overall performance.

For instance, an index fund – a type of mutual fund – that tracks the S&P 500 provides exposure to 500 of the largest U.S. companies. By investing in this fund, you're essentially betting on the collective growth of these companies, which has historically averaged around a 7% annual return. The catch with mutual funds is that they charge fees and expenses, so it's essential to research the fund's expenses before investing. The good news is, many platforms like Fidelity and Vanguard offer low-cost index funds.

Real-Life Example - Balancing a Portfolio

Let's tie this together with a real-life example. Consider Sarah, who is in her early 30s and newly interested in investing. Sarah decides to invest $500 a month. She allocates 60% to stocks, 30% to bonds, and 10% to a mutual fund. Over ten years, with an average return of 7% from stocks, 3% from bonds, and 5% from the mutual fund, Sarah sees substantial growth in her portfolio. Here's a simple breakdown -

- **Stocks (60% at 7% annual return) -** $500 x 0.60 = $300/month, growing to roughly $52,228 in ten years.
- **Bonds (30% at 3% annual return) -** $500 x 0.30 = $150/month, growing to about $21,014 in ten years.
- **Mutual Funds (10% at 5% annual return) -** $500 x 0.10 = $50/month, growing to approximately $7,796 in ten years.

Understanding Investment Risks

Investing always comes with risks, but these can be managed. One way to handle risk is diversification—spreading your investments across different asset classes. Another is to start with smaller amounts to get comfortable. Emotional resilience is also important. Back to Sarah, she experienced market downturns but stayed the course, avoiding panic selling. Her patience paid off, as her portfolio rebounded and continued to grow.

Behavioral finance tells us that informed investors tend to make better decisions. Keep learning and stay updated with financial news. For example, Daniel Kahneman's study on investment psychology highlights that overconfidence can lead to poor investment choices. By being aware of this, Sarah avoids making hasty decisions based on market noise. Investing doesn't need to be intimidating. Start small, stay informed, and watch your wealth grow steadily over time.

Chapter 5 – Planning for Retirement

Imagine standing at the edge of a vast, sunlit valley, filled with possibilities. This is where your retirement stands—a time to embrace freedom from work and enjoy life's simple pleasures. Planning for it is just as crucial as saving for it. Learning how to navigate this journey gives you the tools to shape your future. In this introduction, we will explore the pillars of effective retirement planning. Together, we will unveil what everyone should know to ensure that their golden years truly shine.

It's not just about saving; it's about growing your wealth. Consider the **rule of 72**—a simple formula to estimate how quickly your money will double. If your investment earns 6% annually, it will take roughly 12 years for your money to double (72 divided by 6). Imagine starting with $10,000; in 12 years, you can see it grow to $20,000, and that's before you add any additional savings! This is why one must be strategic about where they invest.

Visualize how you want to spend your days. Will you travel? Pursue hobbies? Or perhaps focus on spending time with family? Once you have clarity, you can estimate how much you'll need. For example, let's say you plan to spend about $5,000 a month. That translates to about $60,000 a year. If you envision a 30-year retirement, you're looking at $1.8 million. This number helps ground your planning efforts.

As we traverse through this chapter, remember - efficient retirement planning isn't merely about accumulating wealth. It's about acquiring the confidence to protect your lifestyle and embrace the life you've dreamt of. By gaining insights into your financial needs, understanding your options, and effectively managing your investments, you will pave the way to a fulfilling retirement. Ready to dig deeper?

Types of Retirement Accounts

401(k) Plans

Let's dive deeper into one of the most powerful tools available for retirement planning—the 401(k) plan. Imagine it as your personal financial vault, where you can deposit your hard-earned money with tax advantages and a potential employer matching that can supercharge your savings. Many employees overlook this gem simply because they don't fully understand it. But once you know the ins and outs, you can turn the 401(k) into a formidable ally for your retirement journey.

A 401(k) plan is an employer-sponsored retirement account that lets you save money before taxes. This means your contributions are deducted from your paycheck, lowering your taxable income. For instance, if you earn $60,000 a year and contribute $6,000 to your 401(k), you'll only be taxed on $54,000. This tax deferral gives you more money to invest and can significantly enhance your growth potential over time.

One of the best features of many 401(k) plans is employer matching. This is essentially free money. If your employer offers a match, take it! For example, if your employer matches up to 5% of your salary and you earn $60,000, that's another $3,000 added to your account! Let's say you consistently contribute that same $6,000 annually, and with an average return of 7%, your 401(k) could grow to over $1 million by the time you retire. It's like finding extra cash in your pocket.

The IRS sets contribution limits for 401(k) plans. In 2024, you can contribute up to $23,000 if you're under 50. If you're 50 or older, there's a catch-up provision that allows you to contribute an extra $8,000. Maxing out your contributions, especially when you consider the compounding interest, can set you on a trajectory for financial security in retirement. If you consistently max out at $23,000 for 20 years with an average 7% return, you could amass over $900,000 by retirement.

When you enroll in your 401(k), you often get to choose how your contributions are invested. Most plans offer a range of options, including stock mutual funds, bond funds, and money market accounts. Look for funds with low expense ratios. They eat into your returns. A fund charging 1.5% may not seem significant annually, but over 30 years, that could cost you hundreds of thousands of dollars.

While you may have the option to take loans or hardship withdrawals, proceed with caution. Loans need to be repaid with interest, and if you leave your job, the loan often becomes due. Withdrawing early can incur steep penalties and taxes. It's like taking a detour on a road trip; it may seem quick but often delays your entire journey.

Roth vs. Traditional - Choosing the Right Path

When pondering your retirement savings, understanding the difference between a Roth IRA and a Traditional IRA is key. It's like choosing between two roads to a beautiful destination. Each path has its benefits, and the right choice depends on your financial goals. Let's break down these options, digging into what each provides and how they fit into your overall retirement strategy.

Roth IRA - A Tax-Free Future

A Roth IRA allows you to contribute after-tax income. This means the money you put in has already been taxed. The beauty of this account lies in its potential - your contributions grow tax-free. When you retire, if you withdraw from your Roth account, those withdrawals are also tax-free, assuming you've met the requirements. This can be incredibly beneficial if you expect to be in a higher tax bracket during retirement.

For instance, let's say you contribute $5,000 annually to a Roth IRA over 30 years, with an average annual return of 7%. By the end of those 30 years, your contributions will have grown to approximately $512,000. When you withdraw that money, it's entirely yours—no taxes to pay. This can feel like winning a lottery where you keep every dollar, allowing you to enjoy your retirement without tax burdens.

Traditional IRA - Immediate Tax Savings

In contrast, a Traditional IRA offers tax-deductible contributions. This means you can reduce your taxable income in the year you contribute. If you earn $70,000 and contribute $6,000 to a Traditional IRA, you'll be taxed only on $64,000. This instant tax break feels like a nice bonus. Over time, your money grows tax deferred. However, when you withdraw funds during retirement, you will pay ordinary income tax on those amounts.

Consider this - if you were to contribute $6,000 annually to a Traditional IRA for 30 years at the same 7% return, you could see a total of around $628,000 by retirement. But remember, when you withdraw this amount, you'll owe taxes on it. If you're in the 20% tax bracket at that time, you'll need to set aside around $125,600 for taxes. So, while the upfront deduction is appealing, it's essential to consider the long-term tax implications.

Your choice between a Roth and a Traditional IRA should hinge on your current and anticipated future tax situation. Think of it as investing in a potion - with the Roth, you know all the ingredients up-front. You pay your dues now and can indulge freely later. With the Traditional, you're deferring some of the costs, but that could mean a hefty bill when you decide to cash in.

To put this in perspective, if you expect your income—and therefore your tax bracket—to rise in the future, a Roth may serve you better. Conversely, if you anticipate a lower tax bracket after retiring, a Traditional IRA could be more advantageous. It's all about what fits your unique financial picture.

The Caveats

While both accounts have their benefits, they are not one-size-fits-all. Each has eligibility requirements and contribution limits. For example, in 2024, the maximum contribution limits for both accounts are $7,000(or $8,000 if you're over 50). But the Roth IRA has income limits. If you earn too much, your ability to contribute phases out. That's where knowing the rules becomes crucial.

Additionally, thoughtful planning is essential. If you find yourself switching back and forth

between these accounts, it can lead to confusion
or even costly mistakes.

In summary, understanding the distinction
between a Roth IRA and a Traditional IRA is not
just a matter of tax strategy. It's a foundation
for your overall retirement planning. By taking
the time to weigh your options, you empower
yourself with the knowledge to make informed
decisions. So, dive into your finances! Analyze
your income, project your future needs, and
map out a path that suits your vision for
retirement.

Other Retirement Accounts

Retirement planning isn't just about 401(k)s
and IRAs. It's a bigger picture. There are other
accounts that may fit your needs perfectly. Each
option has unique features and benefits.
Knowing these can expand your financial toolkit
and push you closer to achieving your
retirement dreams.

SEP IRA - A Simple Option for the Self-Employed

If you're self-employed or own a small business,
consider a **SEP IRA**. This account allows you to
set aside a significant portion of your income
for retirement. For 2024, you can contribute up

to 25% of your net earnings. However, the maximum contribution is capped at **$68,000**. Imagine you net $100,000 as a sole proprietor. You could contribute up to **$25,000**, directly lowering your taxable income while securing your future.

The beauty of the SEP IRA lies in its simplicity. There's minimal paperwork and lower administrative costs compared to other retirement accounts. Contribution flexibility is another perk. You can adjust how much you contribute each year based on your income. Some years you may contribute the maximum, while in leaner years, you can contribute less or nothing at all. This versatility allows you to weather the ups and downs of self-employment.

SIMPLE IRA - An Accessible Choice for Small Businesses

The **SIMPLE IRA** is another excellent option, particularly for small businesses with up to 100 employees. This plan is straightforward to set up and maintain. Employees can contribute up to **$15,500** in 2024, with an additional **$3,500** if they are age 50 or older. If you have employees, your business must either match their contributions up to 3% of their salary or make a 2% non-elective contribution for all eligible employees.

Let's say you run a small firm with three employees who each earn an average salary of **$50,000**. If you choose the matching option, your business will pay **$4,500** in matches for each employee who contributes, helping you build a motivated team while contributing toward their financial well-being.

403(b) Plans - Education and Health Care Professionals

If you work for a public school or a not-for-profit, a **403(b) plan** might be available to you. This plan functions similarly to a 401(k), allowing you to save for retirement using pre-tax dollars. The contribution limits for 403(b) accounts mirror those of 401(k) accounts, which means a potential of **$22,500** for 2024 (or **$30,000** if you are 50 or older).

These plans may also offer additional features like loans and hardship withdrawals. If an unexpected expense arises, you won't have to completely deplete your savings. Use this flexibility wisely—while it can provide quick access to cash, it's essential to remember that it may impact your long-term retirement goals.

457 Plans - For Government Employees

For state and local government employees, there's the **457 plan**. Much like a 401(k), these plans allow you to set aside a portion of your paycheck for retirement. The contribution limits are consistent with 401(k)s, giving you up to **$22,500** in 2024 and an additional catch-up option if you're over 50.

One significant advantage of a 457 plan is the ability to withdraw funds in retirement without incurring an early distribution penalty, even if you're under 59½. This feature can be especially beneficial if your retirement plan includes a transition into a lower income for a few years. However, remember this plan also comes with taxable distributions upon withdrawal.

The Bigger Picture

These accounts provide more ways to build your retirement savings. Understanding your financial situation will help you choose the best option. It's like tailoring a suit—it should fit you perfectly. Each account has its eligibility requirements and contribution limits. Take time to explore your choices and how they align with your goals.

Employer-Sponsored Plans

Understanding employer-sponsored retirement plans is crucial for solid financial planning. These plans can significantly enhance your retirement savings. Employers often provide these accounts not just as a benefit, but as a pathway to grow your investments. When you engage with these plans, you can potentially unlock a treasure trove of financial resources.

Maximizing Employer Contributions

Taking full advantage of employer matching contributions is like discovering free money. Many employers will match your contributions up to a certain percentage. For example, if your company matches 100% of your contributions up to 5% of your salary, this means that if you earn **$50,000** annually and contribute **$2,500**, your employer will add another **$2,500**. That's an instant **50% increase** in your retirement account. It's essential to contribute enough to capture the full match. Not doing so is akin to leaving money on the table.

Understanding your employer's vesting schedule is equally important. This schedule determines how quickly you gain ownership of the employer's contributions. If you switch jobs too soon, you might walk away empty-handed. For instance, with cliff vesting, you might only gain ownership after three years of service. In contrast, graded vesting allows you to take ownership over a period of years. Knowing this can improve your planning as you decide whether to stay or move on.

Understanding Vesting Schedules

Vesting schedules can feel like a puzzle you need to solve. They define how much of the employer's contributions you own over time. A cliff vesting schedule means you get full ownership after a specific period, say three years. If you leave before that, you lose everything. Each of those years is like a countdown. Graded vesting offers a gentler approach. You may own 20% each year until you hit full ownership after five years.

So, what does this look like in reality? If your employer contributes **$10,000** into your retirement fund but you leave after two years with a cliff vesting policy, you walk away with **$0**. But with graded vesting, you would leave with **$4,000**. This becomes crucial when considering moving jobs. Knowing how the vesting works can influence your decisions and help you maximize your benefits.

Taking Control of Your Retirement Strategy

Employer-sponsored plans can form the foundation of your retirement strategy. But it's essential to actively engage with them. Regularly check your contributions. Increase them as your income rises. You might allocate a small bonus or raise directly into your retirement fund. This way, you enhance your savings without feeling the pinch of a reduced paycheck. Imagine treating your retirement as a "pay yourself first" approach.

It's not just about contributing. Keep an eye on the performance of your investments within these plans. If you notice poor returns, don't hesitate to explore other options. Switching funds or reallocating your investments based on risk tolerance could lead to more significant gains. It requires some effort, but the rewards can be substantial.

Retirement Investment Strategies

Investing for retirement is more than just setting aside money. It's about making your savings work hard for you. Many people defer this important task while focusing on daily expenses. However, the sooner you start, the more time your money has to grow. Time is your ally. Think of your retirement strategy as a recipe. Each ingredient must complement the others for the best flavor.

Asset Allocation

The foundation of your retirement strategy hinges on *asset allocation*. This means determining how to spread your investments across various asset classes—like stocks, bonds, and cash. Each class behaves differently under market pressures. Stocks can be volatile but offer growth potential. Bonds tend to be more stable but provide lower returns. Cash is safe but generates minimal interest.

Consider a 30-year-old investor with a long retirement horizon. They might allocate **80%** of their portfolio to stocks and **20%** to bonds. As they age, they could gradually shift towards bonds, perhaps going for **60%** stocks and **40%** bonds by the time they reach 50. This strategy adjusts the risk based on how close they are to retirement.

Rebalancing

Now that you've allocated your assets, it's critical to **rebalance** them regularly. This means adjusting your investments to maintain your desired allocation. Let's say your portfolio initially had **80%** in stocks. Over time, due to market performance, it might shift to **90%** in stocks and **10%** in bonds. To rebalance, you would sell some stocks and buy more bonds to return to your target.

Expert recommendations suggest reviewing your portfolio at least once a year. During this time, you can assess how your investments are performing. Consider sales during major market fluctuations. For instance, if you see a tech stock surge while others lag, it may be time to sell a portion of the successful investment and reinvest in underperforming sectors. This strategy helps manage risk and aligns your portfolio back to your goals.

Long-Term Growth

Long-term growth hinges on investments that have the potential to appreciate significantly. Stocks typically offer this growth but come with risks. Focus on *growth-oriented mutual funds* and companies with solid fundamentals. For example, if you invest **$5,000** in a mutual fund with an average annual return of **8%**, it could grow to approximately **$10,000** in just nine years. This emphasizes the power of *compound interest*.

Understand the difference between impulse and informed investing. Avoid the trap of following trends. Instead, rely on thorough research and analysis. Successful companies often showcase significant market share and innovative products. Look for those that consistently perform well and have a positive outlook.

Tax Considerations

Tax Advantages of Retirement Accounts

Retirement accounts come with powerful tax benefits. These advantages can turn your savings strategy into a profitable journey.

1. **Pre-tax Contributions** - When you contribute to accounts like a traditional IRA or 401(k), you lower your taxable income for the year. For example, if you earn $80,000 and contribute $5,000 pre-tax, your taxable income drops to $75,000. This can place you in a lower tax bracket.

2. **Tax-deferred Growth** - Imagine your investments growing without the taxman knocking on your door. In a tax-deferred account, you won't pay taxes on earnings until you withdraw funds. If you start with $10,000 and achieve an average

return of 7% over 20 years, your account could grow to around $38,696 by the end of that period—all without taxes taking a slice along the way.

3. **Tax-free Withdrawals with Roth Accounts** - With a Roth IRA, you pay taxes on your contributions now. But when you retire, you can withdraw money tax-free. If you contribute $5,000 annually to a Roth for 30 years and see it grow to $400,000 by age 65, you won't owe a penny on those withdrawals. That money is all yours.

Required Minimum Distributions (RMDs)

Start thinking about Required Minimum Distributions when you hit age 72. The government wants a slice of your retirement pie, so you must start withdrawing from traditional IRAs and 401(k) plans. Ignoring this rule leads to hefty penalties—up to 50% on your RMD. So, if you should have withdrawn $10,000 and didn't, you could face a $5,000 penalty.

RMDs are calculated based on your account balance and life expectancy. This means the balance you've carefully built still affects your tax situation in retirement. Consider working with a financial advisor to strategize your withdrawals effectively. This can help you manage your tax burden when the time comes.

Real-Life Examples

Let's take a page from Sarah's story. Sarah decides to contribute 10% of her $60,000 salary to her 401(k). That's $6,000 a year. Employers often match contributions, which is free money!

In Sarah's case, her employer matches 50% on contributions up to 6%. So, when she contributes $3,600 (6% of her salary), her employer adds another $1,800. This brings her total annual contribution to $7,800. Over 35 years, assuming a 7% average return, Sarah's nest egg could grow to approximately $1,062,000. That's a considerable reward for merely taking full advantage of her employer's match.

On the other hand, John earns a solid $120,000 a year. He takes advantage of tax-free growth by maxing out both a Roth IRA and a Traditional IRA. For the year 2024, he can contribute up to $7,000 to each, plus an additional $1,000 if he's over 50. So, with both accounts, he can contribute $16,000 annually.

With a 7% average return, John's combined contributions can balloon to about $1,065,000 over 30 years. Using both accounts allows him to benefit from tax diversification in retirement—paying taxes on some money now and having other funds grow tax-free for his later years.

Now, let's look at Emma. She starts investing at 23, committing $500 monthly to a Roth IRA. That's $6,000 a year. With a consistent 7% return, Emma could see her contributions blossom into around $1,240,000 by age 65. This highlights the power of time and compound interest.

Every dollar you save today can multiply over the years. Your tax considerations play a critical role in this equation, making it essential to understand how taxes will impact your future.

Chapter 6 – Planning for Your Children's Future

Every parent wishes for their child to have the best possible opportunities. A key element of giving your children that advantage is understanding the various savings options available to you. College can be a hefty expense, with the average public university tuition sitting around $10,000 per year and private institutions often exceeding $35,000. Without a clear plan, this daunting figure can feel overwhelming. This is where financial planning comes in. Establishing savings early can help buffer the burden and ensure your children have the resources they need when they step onto campus.

As a parent, the responsibility may feel weighty. The key is to start small, remain consistent, and watch how your planning transforms their future. Picture a sculptor chiseling away a block of marble into a beautiful statue. Each contribution and savings decision is a careful strike, shaping your child's financial future. With the right strategies in place, you create a path filled with opportunities and possibilities.

In the upcoming sections, we will explore these savings options in depth. You will learn how to select the right plan, how to set achievable goals, and strategies to keep your savings on track. The journey may seem daunting, but with the right tools and information, you can confidently navigate the financial landscape for your child's future. Financial empowerment is all about making informed decisions now, ensuring that your children can soar when the time comes.

Understanding College Savings Plans

When it comes to saving for your child's education, establishing a solid plan can feel as critical as building a sturdy foundation for a house. You wouldn't want to start construction on shaky ground, and similarly, saving without a structured approach can lead to uncertainty. Let's dive deeper into the ins and outs of college savings plans, particularly the ever-popular 529 plans. These are designed specifically to ease the financial burden of college costs when the time comes.

First, let's talk about the **tax advantages**. With a 529 plan, your contributions grow *tax-free*. This means you won't pay taxes on the earnings as they accumulate. When your child heads off to college, you can withdraw the money to pay for qualified education expenses, again without incurring taxes. This benefit can save you hundreds, if not thousands, of dollars. For instance, if you contribute $10,000 today and it grows to $15,000 in ten years, you get to use that entire $15,000 for education expenses without a tax burden.

Next is **flexibility**. Funds from a 529 plan can be used for a range of education costs—not just tuition. This includes textbooks, supplies, and even room and board. Imagine covering your child's new laptop or that hefty textbook bill without pangs of financial regret. Who doesn't want that?

It's also essential to consider the **high contribution limits**. Most 529 plans allow you to contribute substantial amounts, often exceeding $300,000 over the life of the account. This is key for those who might aim for a private university that can exceed $50,000 annually by the time your child is ready to enroll.

Diving into Plan Types

There are primarily two types of 529 plans.

1. **Prepaid Tuition Plans** - These plans let you lock in tuition at current rates. If tuition costs rise by 5% annually, and today's rates are $10,000, your prepaid contract means you pay that amount now, ensuring your child's tuition stays at $10,000, even if it skyrockets in the future.

2. **Education Savings Plans** - These function more like traditional investment accounts. You can invest contributions in various mutual funds or other securities. If invested wisely, they can grow significantly based on market performance, much like your retirement account. For example, if a plan grows at an average annual return of 7%, a $15,000 contribution can swell to about $30,000 in just ten years. But remember, market performance fluctuates, meaning there is some risk involved.

Selecting the right 529 plan takes research but is crucial for maximizing savings. Look closely at state-sponsored options. Some states offer tax deductions or credits for contributions. For instance, if you live in Ohio and contribute $4,000 to your 529 plan, you may receive a tax deduction, reducing your taxable income for that year.

Comparing fees among different plans is also vital. These can eat into your savings. If one plan charges a fee of 1% and another charges 0.5%, the savings can add up over time.

As you take these steps, think about your **financial goals**. Set short-term and long-term objectives. Perhaps you want your child to attend a specific university. How much total funding will you need? Break that down to yearly contributions. If you aim to save $100,000 in 15 years, you'll need to set aside approximately $5,556 each year.

Savings Accounts for Children

Building your child's financial future starts with a simple yet powerful tool—a savings account. It's like laying out a solid path toward financial literacy while simultaneously creating a safety net for their money. Beginning this journey early can instill valuable habits that last a lifetime.

Opening a savings account is typically an easy process. You'll find most banks offer child-friendly options with minimal requirements. Look for accounts that have no minimum balance. You want to make this as accessible as possible. Some institutions even provide higher interest rates for children's accounts. Why is this important? Higher interest helps your child's savings grow faster. Imagine if you start with $100; if the account offers 2% interest, in one year, that balance will grow to $102. Though it might seem small at first, those few extra dollars can teach your child about the benefits of saving.

Involve your child in the process of setting up the account. This is when the educational value kicks in. Take them along to the bank. Let them see how banking works. This hands-on experience demystifies money management. Talk about the importance of saving. Discuss how they can use their allowance or gift money to build their account. Setting a schedule for regular deposits will encourage good habits. Perhaps you could agree that for every $10 they save, you'll match their savings with an extra $5. This small incentive teaches them about rewards linked to responsible saving.

As your child engages with their savings account, get them excited about achieving goals. Sharing specific targets adds a layer of motivation. If they want a new bicycle that costs $200, outline the steps to reach this target. For instance, if they save $20 monthly, they will reach that goal in just 10 months. Along the way, remind them how each deposit is one step closer to their dream purchase.

Safety is another critical aspect of savings accounts. Most accounts are FDIC-insured up to $250,000. What does that mean? If the bank were to face any issues, the government guarantees the safety of your child's funds up to that amount. Knowing their savings are secure can instill a sense of confidence and security in your child.

In today's fast-paced environment, financial education is more crucial than ever. A staggering 41% of adults do not maintain a budget. Fostering savings habits early can help your child become part of a growing minority that prioritizes financial discipline. Just as we invest in our children's health and education, we must also invest in their financial savvy.

Creating a habit of saving early equips your child with the skills they need for their financial future. Think of it as building their financial toolkit. Every deposit is like adding a new tool. Over time, they will have everything they need to tackle larger challenges. They'll understand the value of money and the power of saving. Remember, the habits they form now will guide them in adulthood. The earlier you start this journey, the smoother their path will be when they eventually face life's financial decisions.

Certificates of Deposit (CDs)

After establishing a savings account, consider stepping up your child's financial education with Certificates of Deposit (CDs). Think of a CD as a promise. You're agreeing to lock in your money for a predetermined period in exchange for a higher return. This is not just a strategy; it's a tool for growing wealth over time while helping your child learn the value of patience and planning.

One of the immediate benefits of a CD is the higher interest rates typically offered compared to regular savings accounts. For example, while a standard account may offer 0.5% interest, you could find a CD with rates around 2% or more, depending on the term length. Suppose you deposit $1,000 in a 12-month CD at 2%. By the end of that year, you'll have earned $20 in interest, bringing your total to $1,020. That small but significant increase illustrates how time and commitment can yield tangible results. And don't forget, this growth is also FDIC-insured up to $250,000, adding a layer of security to your child's funds.

When selecting the right CD, term length plays a crucial role. Shorter terms, like 6 months, provide flexibility if your child wants to access their funds sooner. However, longer terms, such as 3 or 5 years, generally offer higher rates, rewarding you for leaving your money untouched. Think about your child's saving goals. If they're saving up for a big purchase like a new gaming console, a 12-month CD could be perfectly timed. It allows them to accumulate interest while keeping the goal in sight.

It's also beneficial to shop around. Banks may differ in their rates and terms. Use online comparison tools to find the most attractive offers. For instance, one bank may offer a 3-year CD at 2.5%, while another has a similar product at just 2.0%. Over three years, that difference may seem small, but it can lead to a significant earning potential. You might also find banks offering promotional rates for new accounts or for children's savings specifically, making it an exciting prospect to engage your child in discovering options together.

Consider the psychological aspect of committing to a CD. By agreeing to lock away funds, your child is making a mental shift from immediate gratification to long-term thinking. This can be a powerful life lesson. It lays the groundwork for responsible financial behaviors later. Making this commitment can feel similar to training for a sport; it requires discipline, patience, and a clear goal.

As your child progresses with their CD, share stories about different financial success stories. Case studies of young entrepreneurs or savers who have benefited from holding onto investments can be enlightening. Teach them about famous investors like Warren Buffett, who, despite initial sacrifices, built wealth through patience and strategic planning. Let them understand that the money they save today supports their dreams of tomorrow, be it college, travel, or even starting their own business.

Investment Accounts for Children – Custodial Accounts (UGMA/UTMA)

Building on the principles of saving and investing introduced through certificates of deposit (CDs), custodial accounts present a broader arena for nurturing your child's financial future. These accounts, governed by the Uniform Gifts to Minors Act (UGMA) and the Uniform Transfers to Minors Act (UTMA), provide a unique opportunity to introduce your child to a world of investment. Picture this as giving them a treasure chest filled with possibilities. Instead of simply saving for a rainy day, they can engage with various financial instruments, allowing them to begin their journey toward financial independence early.

How do custodial accounts work? Essentially, you open an account in your child's name. However, until they reach the age of majority—usually 18 or 21—you act as the custodian. This means you manage the account, guiding their investment decisions while they learn the ropes of financial responsibility. For example, if you choose to invest $5,000 in a diversified portfolio of stocks and bonds, your child will not only witness the growth of their investment but also be involved in discussions about which stocks to buy or sell. This hands-on approach can spark their interest in personal finance, helping them make informed choices in the future.

When considering the tax implications of custodial accounts, it's vital to remember that your child's earnings may be taxed at their lower tax rate. This could lead to significant savings compared to if you invested the same amount in your name. For instance, investing in a mutual fund that generates a $500 return could mean a marginal tax rate of only 10% for your child instead of 22% if the investment were in your account. This translates to a tax bill of just $50 instead of $110, allowing your child to retain more of their earnings.

Yet, while custodial accounts come with many advantages, they also have their challenges. Upon reaching adulthood, your child gains full control of the funds. This can be a double-edged sword. You may have invested with the hope they would use the money wisely, perhaps for education or starting a business. However, the sudden access to funds might lead to less prudent spending choices. It's essential to prepare them for this transition. Discuss setting goals. Explain how to create a budget. Share stories of young adults who responsibly managed their newfound wealth and those who did not.

Another point to consider is the flexibility of these accounts. Unlike CDs, which can restrict access to funds for a set period, custodial accounts allow you to use the money to benefit your child in various ways. Want to cover their summer camp fees or contribute to their first car? These accounts can facilitate those dreams directly. Picture this - your child's 16th birthday is approaching. Instead of merely handing over some cash, you can invest in a custodial account and discuss how the money accrued there can help fund their driving lessons or the purchase of that first vehicle.

When contemplating investing in custodial accounts, think about your own financial philosophy. Are you an aggressive investor willing to take on risks, or do you favor a conservative approach? Tailor your investment strategy to align with your child's personality and life goals. Perhaps an exploration of index funds might resonate with them more than individual stocks, which can be volatile.

Teaching Financial Literacy to Children

Now that we've explored custodial accounts, let's shift gears and delve deeper into the essential skill of teaching financial literacy to children. Like a sturdy bridge, financial literacy supports your child's journey to adulthood. To prepare them for this path, start with **age-appropriate learning**. For younger children, consider using playful methods. You might hand them a piggy bank, fostering an early instinct to save.

Watch how their eyes light up when they feed coins into it. For older children, incorporate more substantial concepts like budgeting. Introduce them to simple spreadsheets or apps that track their spending. Encourage them to set up a mock budget for an upcoming family outing. This way, they'll understand the real-world implications of their choices.

Next, involve them in your family financial planning sessions. Many parents might shy away from discussing budgets at home, fearing it's too complex for kids. But think back to that first time you let your child pick the menu for a family dinner. They love having a say! When you set a budget for groceries, encourage your children to help make choices. Ask them to find the best deals or suggest meals that fit within the limit. By doing this, they learn the value of money been spent wisely. Now let's consider some numbers. For instance, if your weekly grocery budget is $150, explain how staying within that budget means no last-minute purchases at the corner store, sparing you that extra $20.

To enhance their learning, leverage resources and tools that make finances engaging. The world is rife with educational apps designed for this very purpose. Apps like *Greenlight* or

GoHenry allow your child to manage their own debit card in a safe environment. Picture them visiting their favorite store, using their card while understanding how to track their spending. It's an empowering experience. Combine this with books tailored for their age group. Titles like *The Everything Kids' Money Book* and *Adesua's Big Adventure: Learning About Money* provide insights that promote curiosity about finances.

At times, it's beneficial to share stories. Perhaps you've faced financial challenges that required learning along the way. Don't hesitate to share these experiences with your children. Relate your tales of financial errors and victories. For example, if you once overspent on a holiday shopping spree, take those lessons and craft them into relatable stories. Connecting real-life scenarios can often resonate more deeply than abstract concepts. Children might remember your experience with overspending for years, and it might influence their choices when they're in similar situations.

Also, instill a sense of goal setting. Just like preparing for a race, having a target gives purpose. Have your child articulate their savings goals. Maybe they want a new bike costing $300. By breaking this down into smaller milestones, like saving \$30 each month, it becomes more achievable. They will begin to grasp that financial goals require dedication and a bit of foresight.

Ultimately, teaching financial literacy is not a one-off conversation. It's an ongoing journey. The more you involve your children in financial decisions, the more comfortable they will be discussing money openly in the future.

As their understanding grows, they become equipped with the knowledge and skills to navigate financial challenges effectively. In this way, you're not just setting them up for responsible financial habits; you're empowering them for life.

Chapter 7 – Managing Debt

You may feel overwhelmed or even intimidated when you hear the word 'debt.' However, understanding it is the first step towards taking control of your financial future. Debt can be a tool or a trap. In this chapter, we're going to explore how different types of debt behave and how to manage them effectively. It's essential to know that you are not alone in this journey. Take a deep breath. Let's dive in.

First, let's break down the types of debt. Think of credit card debt as a hungry monster. It can devour your finances if not managed properly. With interest rates averaging around 18%, making just the minimum payment can take years to pay off. Imagine you owe $5,000 on your credit card and you only pay the minimum of $100 a month. At this rate, you'll be in a cycle of debt for over five years and pay almost $2,200 in interest alone! When you pay more than the minimum whenever possible. This will slice through that monster's appetite quickly.

Next up, student loans. These can feel like a necessary evil but can also offer flexibility.

Federal student loans have lower interest rates, typically between 4% and 7%, depending on the type of loan. They allow for deferment and income-driven repayment plans, which can make life easier if you're struggling to find a job post-graduation. Let's say you borrowed $30,000 at 5% interest. If you opt for a standard 10-year plan, your monthly payments will be around $318.

Mortgages are the long-term commitments you hear about so often. They often have lower interest rates—around 3% to 4%—but purchasing a home represents a huge financial burden. Consider a $300,000 home with a 4% interest rate over 30 years. Your monthly payment will be about $1,432. Not too terrible, right? But you'll end up paying nearly $215,000 in interest over the life of the loan!

Lastly, we have personal loans. These can vary significantly in both terms and interest rates. Some might be as low as 5%, while others could skyrocket to 36%. It's essential to shop around and read the fine print before signing anything. For instance, a $10,000 loan at 15% interest for 5 years leads to a monthly payment of around $239 and will cost you about $3,400 in interest. Always calculate the total loan cost.

In this chapter, we'll explore strategies for paying off debt efficiently. Careful planning and budgeting can help you stay on track while managing your debt effectively. Let's take control together!

Strategies for Paying Off Debt Efficiently

Now that we've broken down the different types of debt, it's time to tackle the strategies that can help you pay it off effectively. Think of managing debt like climbing a mountain. The path can be steep and challenging. But with the right tools and techniques, you can reach the summit. Let's explore the methods that will empower you to take control of your finances.

First, let's talk about the Snowball Method. This approach is all about momentum. You start by focusing on your smallest debts. Picture this - you owe four debts. One is a small credit card bill of $500. Another is a personal loan of $2,000. Next is a larger credit card balance of $4,000 and finally, a $10,000 student loan. By tackling that $500 debt first, you clear it quickly. The sense of accomplishment bolsters your morale. It's like finishing a warm-up lap before a race. You gain momentum. Once the smallest debt is paid off, apply the same payments to the next smallest. You'll build confidence along the way, which is crucial in this journey.

Alternatively, you can consider the Avalanche Method. This strategy is all about saving money. You prioritize your debts based on interest rates. Imagine you have those same four debts. The credit card with a 23% interest rate takes precedence over the others. By paying it off first, you save more in interest costs. For example, paying down a $4,000 credit card at that rate could save you $1,000 or more in interest compared to tackling lower-interest debts first. The Avalanche Method requires discipline but pays off in the long run. It is a logical approach that lets you tackle the most costly debt head-on.

Then there's debt consolidation and refinancing. These are valuable tools. Consider you have multiple debts with various interest rates. By consolidating them into one loan, you can often secure a lower rate. This can simplify your payments from several due dates to just one. Let's say you've accumulated $15,000 across various cards with an average interest rate of 18%.

By consolidating into a personal loan at 10% interest, you not only lower your monthly payments but also save over $2,500 in interest over the life of your loan. Remember, however, that not every consolidation or refinancing opportunity is beneficial. Always check the terms before making a move.

Lastly, don't forget about budgeting. This isn't just a boring spreadsheet; it's an empowering exercise. Start by listing your income and expenses. Track where your money goes every month. This clarity helps you identify areas you can cut back on. Even a $50 monthly restaurant budget, when redirected to debt, can drastically alter your repayment timeline. If you apply that $50 extra to a $5,000 credit card debt at 18% interest, you'll pay it off nearly a year earlier!

To sum it up, there are various methods to handle debt, each with its own merits. Whether you choose the Snowball, Avalanche, or consolidation approach, remember that the most important step is to take action. Each dollar you direct towards your debt brings you closer to financial freedom. Like reaching the peak after a challenging climb, the satisfaction of being debt-free is worth the effort. So, gather your strategies and let's tackle that mountain together!

Chapter 8 – Tax Planning and Strategies

When it comes to your finances, taxes can often feel like a shadow lurking in the background. They are never far away and sometimes they can be downright confusing. Picture taxes as a large puzzle. When you know how the pieces fit together, the picture becomes a lot clearer, and you'll be better equipped to reduce your overall tax bill.

First things first, you need to know your tax bracket. This determines how much of your income you owe to the government. For instance, if your income falls into the 22% tax bracket, that means you pay 22% on the income within that range, not on your entire income. Understanding your bracket can help you make more informed decisions about extra earnings or investments. For example, let's say you earn $50,000 a year and receive a $5,000 bonus. That bonus might push you into a higher bracket, costing you more in taxes. Planning around this could save you a lot.

Knowing what and how to deduct can also make a big difference. By the end of this chapter, you will walk away with actionable strategies to help you navigate the world of taxes more effectively. Our goal is to make these financial responsibilities feel less like a chore and more like an opportunity.

Let's arm you with the knowledge to transform tax season from a dreaded experience to a chance to celebrate your financial progress!

Tax-Advantaged Accounts

When it comes to managing your taxes, understanding tax-advantaged accounts is like having a secret weapon in your financial toolkit. These accounts not only help you save money but also lower your taxable income. By using them wisely, you can transform your tax obligations into opportunities for growth.

Health Savings Accounts (HSAs)

Let's start with Health Savings Accounts (HSAs). These accounts allow you to contribute pre-tax dollars that can be used for qualified medical expenses. Think of HSAs as a piggy bank for your healthcare costs. Contributions are tax-deductible and when you withdraw the money for eligible expenses, it's tax-free. For example, if you set aside $3,000 in an HSA this year and use it for medical bills, you just saved tax dollars on the income you contributed. If you're in the 22% tax bracket, that means you effectively saved $660 on your taxes this year. Plus, many HSAs offer a way to invest those funds, giving you a chance to grow your savings.

Flexible Spending Accounts (FSAs)

Next up are Flexible Spending Accounts (FSAs). They work similarly to HSAs by allowing you to use pre-tax dollars for medical and dependent care expenses. The difference? FSAs typically come with a use-it-or-lose-it rule. If you contribute $2,500 to an FSA but only use $2,000, you may forfeit the remaining balance at the end of the plan year. It's important to plan carefully. Imagine you're preparing for a big expense like your child's daycare or an upcoming surgery. Knowing how much to contribute can help you make the most of these accounts while avoiding any waste.

Minimizing Tax Liability

Understanding tax liability doesn't have to be daunting. With the right strategies, you can feel empowered and in control of your financial future. Think of minimizing taxes like navigating a maze. With a map in hand, you can find the best paths to success without running into dead ends. Let's explore key strategies that everyone should know about.

Deductions and Tax Credits

Deductions are powerful tools for lowering your taxable income. They come in several forms but focus on the ones that resonate with you. For instance, mortgage interest can significantly decrease your taxable income. Assume you pay $12,000 in mortgage interest annually. If you fall within the 22% tax bracket, that deduction saves you $2,640 on your tax bill. Charitable donations also deserve your attention. If you give $1,000 to your local charity, that's a dollar-for-dollar reduction in your taxable income.

Now, turn your eyes toward tax credits. Unlike deductions, which reduce income, credits reduce the taxes you owe directly. The Earned Income Tax Credit (EITC) is an excellent example. If you qualify, it can provide a credit of up to $6,728 based on your income and number of dependents. That can mean the difference between financial strain and a well-earned relief.

Efficient Tax Planning

Being proactive is crucial. Start planning your financial moves at least a year in advance. Consider how income-generating activities might land you in a higher tax bracket. If you've got a side hustle or investment income, strategize. Say you expect to earn an additional $10,000 this year. If that takes you over the threshold for the 24% tax bracket, you'll be paying more taxes than necessary.

To sidestep this pitfall, think about investing in tax-deferred accounts like 401(k)s or IRAs. Contributions made to these accounts are generally tax-deductible, which means you can lower your taxable income now and defer taxes until you withdraw those funds in retirement. If you were to contribute $5,000 to your 401(k), you'd wipe out that additional income for the year, keeping you in a more favorable bracket.

The Power of Record-Keeping

Don't underestimate the power of meticulous records. Keep receipts for every deduction you claim. This can range from business-related costs to medical expenses. Let's say you have $1,200 in receipts for medical expenses not covered by insurance. If they exceed 7.5% of your adjusted gross income, you can deduct the portion exceeding that threshold. If your adjusted gross income is $50,000, you could deduct $600 from your taxes. It's important to document everything. Good records provide you the confidence to claim the deductions you deserve.

Finally, don't shy away from seeking expert advice when necessary. A tax professional can be a valuable asset. They understand the complexities of tax laws and can provide insights that may not be apparent at first glance. They often identify opportunities for deductions or credits that could save you significant sums. Use these strategies to turn tax liabilities into manageable components of your overall financial plan.

Chapter 9 – Insurance and Risk Management

Unexpected events can sweep in like a storm. The right insurance is your shelter, protecting your finances and providing peace of mind.

So, what do you absolutely need to know about insurance? First, understand the basic types - health, life, disability, property, and liability. Health insurance can save you from crippling medical bills. For example, a single hospital visit can cost tens of thousands of dollars. Without insurance, one emergency could wipe out your savings. Life insurance, on the other hand, offers financial stability to your loved ones when you're no longer around. A $500,000 life insurance policy can provide a safety net that covers mortgage payments and living expenses for your family.

Disability insurance is another unsung hero. If you became unable to work due to an accident or illness, how would you pay your bills? For instance, a long-term disability could mean losing out on three to five years of income. A disability policy can replace a significant portion of that lost income, keeping you afloat during tough times. Then there's property insurance, which protects your home and belongings. Imagine a house fire leading to a loss of $200,000 in property; without insurance, you would be left to face that burden alone.

Liability insurance is vital, too. It covers legal costs if someone is injured on your property and sues you. Think about this - if a guest slips and falls, the medical bills could quickly escalate. Having enough liability coverage can be the difference between a financial disaster and a manageable setback.

In this chapter, we will dive deeper into why understanding your coverage is not just about having a policy—it's about having the right one. We'll explore how to determine the coverage you need and how to shop for policies wisely. You'll learn practical strategies that arm you against financial setbacks. It's like an umbrella on a rainy day; you never know when you might need it, but when the storm hits, you'll be glad it's there.

Choosing the Right Coverage

Selecting the right insurance coverage is like finding the perfect safety net for your unique needs. It starts with a clear understanding of your financial landscape. What do you own? What risks are looming? Evaluating your needs is an essential first step. Picture this - you're sitting across from an insurance agent, and you have a list of your assets and dependents on hand. Do you have kids? A house? Significant savings?

These factors will guide you in determining just how much coverage you really need. Think about possible hazards. For example, a homeowner needs enough property insurance to cover not just the house but also furniture, electronics, and personal belongings. If your home were to suffer extensive damage, let's say $150,000, without proper coverage, you'd be digging deep into your savings to recover.

Comparing Policies

Once you've outlined your needs, it's time to shop around. Not all policies are created equal. You will want to compare multiple options. Start by reading the fine print. Focus on what is covered and what is not. Look for exclusions and limitations. For example, some policies may not cover flooding or natural disasters. If you live in a flood zone and have not considered this, you could be leaving yourself open to financial disaster.

Take the time to gather quotes, but also consider the reputation of the insurance provider. A solid company with responsive service can be invaluable when you need to file a claim. A study conducted by J.D. Power found that customers who felt well-informed about their policy were 30% more satisfied with their insurance experience. Understanding what you're buying is crucial, so don't hesitate to ask questions.

The Importance of Coverage Limits

Another critical factor to consider is coverage limits. While a lower premium may be enticing, it usually means a cap on the amount you can claim. This can leave you vulnerable in a significant loss event. For instance, if you pick a policy with a $100,000 limit on property damage, but your home is worth $300,000, you see the potential gap. In the unfortunate event of a total loss, that policy may hardly make a dent in your financial recovery. Always assess your coverage limits against your assets and potential risks.

Insurance is all about balance. You want enough coverage to protect yourself but not so much that you're overpaying. This is where the concept of risk tolerance comes into play. Just as investors weigh potential gains against market volatility, your approach to insurance should consider what you can afford to lose versus what you can manage in premiums. It's like walking a tightrope; too much on either side could lead you to financial instability.

As you dive deeper into insurance and risk management, remember that making informed decisions today sets the stage for financial security tomorrow. By understanding your unique risks and what each policy offers, you're not just buying insurance—you're investing in your peace of mind.

Chapter 10 – Financial Planning for Different Life Stages

Every phase of life brings unique challenges and opportunities. Whether you're a fresh graduate starting your career or approaching retirement, understanding your financial journey is crucial. Think of financial planning like a road trip. Each stop along the way requires different resources, whether it's food, fuel, or a place to sleep. You wouldn't want to run out of gas halfway to your destination, right?

The final chapter is a sum of what we've discussed so far, tailored to different life stages. We'll guide you through the essentials of financial planning for young adults, families, and retirees.

Starting Your Career

Embarking on your career journey is both exhilarating and daunting. You're entering a world filled with opportunities. However, it's vital to establish a solid financial foundation. Think of this phase like setting up a home. You wouldn't start buying furniture before you have a roof over your head, right? In financial terms, this means budgeting and saving before anything else.

Budgeting and Saving

Creating a budget is your first step. This is not just a list of income and expenses. It's a roadmap that guides your spending and saving habits. Aim to track your expenses for at least a month. You might be surprised how much those morning lattes cost when you add them up. After identifying your expenses, prioritize saving.

A good rule of thumb is the 50/30/20 budget - 50% for needs, 30% for wants, and 20% for savings or debts. For instance, if you earn $3,000 monthly, set aside $600 for savings and debt repayment. Start an emergency fund. Aim for at least three to six months' worth of living expenses. This cushion will give you peace of mind during unexpected situations.

Building Credit

A good credit score opens doors. It allows you to rent an apartment or buy a car with better interest rates. Keeping balances low and paying bills on time is essential. Discover what types of credit cards work for you. For example, a secured card is perfect for building credit if you're just starting. Keep your usage under 30% of your limit. That means if your credit limit is $1,000, don't owe more than $300 at any time. Monitoring your credit report regularly keeps you informed. You can get a free report every year. Use it to check for errors and understand your credit standing.

Starting your career involves many choices. They shape not just your professional path but your financial future as well. As you make decisions about spending, saving, and building credit, remember it's all about laying the groundwork. Establishing healthy financial habits now will empower you in all future stages of your life, allowing you to thrive rather than just survive.

By focusing on budgeting and credit, you're not just making ends meet; you're driving toward a bright and secure future.

Growing Your Family

Starting or expanding a family is a thrilling adventure. It brings joy and rewards but comes with financial responsibilities. You want to plan wisely. Think of financial planning during this phase as preparing for a significant event. Just like you would plan for a wedding, you need to lay out the steps for growing your family. Every decision you make now impacts your financial future.

Financial Planning for Marriage

When you tie the knot, merging finances can feel like navigating uncharted waters. It's essential to have transparent conversations about money. Discuss your income, savings, and debts openly. This discussion is the foundation of your financial partnership. Set joint financial goals. What savings do you want to achieve together?

Perhaps it's a down payment on a home or a dream vacation. Create a shared budget that reflects these goals. For example, if your combined monthly income is $5,000, you might decide to allocate $1,500 for savings. This budget should include essential expenses, discretionary spending, and savings for the future.

Planning for Children

Once your family starts to grow, the financial landscape changes dramatically. Children bring immense joy, but they also incur various costs.

Beyond diapers and baby food, consider future expenses like education. Start by saving early. A 529 plan is an excellent tool for this purpose. If you save $200 a month from your child's birth until they turn 18, you could accumulate over $43,000 for education. This plan not only helps you save but also offers tax advantages.

In addition to education, you need to increase your insurance coverage. Life insurance is vital when you have dependents. A good rule of thumb is to have coverage equal to ten times your annual income. For instance, if you earn $60,000 a year, aim for a policy worth $600,000. This ensures your family's financial stability in the event of unforeseen circumstances.

Adjusting Your Budget

As your family grows, your budget should adapt to the new dynamics. Revisit your spending categories regularly. Expenses can change, so stay informed and flexible. Allocate more towards necessities and savings. Using the previous example, if child-related expenses total $1,000 monthly, you will need to ensure your budget accommodates this without straining other areas.

Managing finances as a family is a balancing act. Just as you juggle responsibilities at home, you'll need to juggle your finances with intention. With a clear budget, open communication about money, and a proactive savings strategy, you'll create a solid foundation for your family's future. By focusing on clear goals and adapting to change, you ensure not just survival, but a thriving family life.

Preparing for Retirement

As you mature in life, retirement planning becomes a critical focus. It's not just about saving; it's about ensuring a comfortable future. Think of retirement as crossing a bridge. You want to be sure it's sturdy enough to carry you and your plans without a hitch. Planning ahead prepares you for the unexpected.

Strategies for Later Starters

If you're starting to plan for retirement a bit late, don't worry—you're not alone. Many people find themselves in this position. The key is to maximize your retirement contributions. If you can contribute to a 401(k) or an IRA, aim to put in the maximum allowable amount. For instance, if you are under 50, the current limit for a 401(k) is $22,500. If you're over 50, you can add an extra $7,500 as a catch-up contribution.

This can significantly increase your retirement savings over time.

Next, tackle any existing debts. High-interest debts can cripple your financial freedom. Aim to pay off credit cards first. If you owe $5,000 on a card with an 18% interest rate, focusing your payments there saves you hundreds in interest long-term.

Finally, reassess your financial goals regularly. What do you want retirement to look like? Visualize it vividly. Do you see yourself travelling or enjoying time with family? Knowing this helps you set realistic savings targets.

Creating a Retirement Plan

Start by estimating your retirement expenses. Consider elements like housing, healthcare, and lifestyle. A typical rule of thumb suggests you'll need about 70-80% of your pre-retirement income in retirement. So, if you currently earn $60,000, plan for around $42,000 to $48,000 annually. But don't just guess. Get specific. Calculate what you'll spend on healthcare. Did you know that, on average, a couple will need approximately $315,000 to cover healthcare costs? This figure can catch you off guard if unprepared.

Potential income sources must also be calculated. Social Security might not be as generous as you think. As of 2024, the average monthly benefit is about $1,800. Factor this in and determine how much you will need to save to fill the gap.

Investing wisely is paramount. Your portfolio should be diversified. This involves spreading your investments across various asset classes. Stocks, bonds, and real estate make a robust mix. If you're uncomfortable making these decisions, consider speaking with a financial advisor.

Withdrawing funds sustainably is another aspect often overlooked. Your withdrawal rate should ideally fall between 4-5% annually. This strategy helps ensure your funds last throughout retirement. For example, if you retire with $500,000, a 4% withdrawal allows you to take out $20,000 each year without running out of money too quickly.

Retirement planning may feel daunting, but taking small, actionable steps can guide you. Always keep your goals in sight like a focused athlete on the track. Monitor your progress and adjust as life evolves. Keep in mind that retirement is a journey, not just a destination.

Planning wisely today sets the stage for enjoyment in your later years. Dive in headfirst and embrace your financial future with confidence!

Parting Words

As we wrap up our journey, I want you to remember that building generational wealth isn't just about amassing money. It's about fostering a mindset of growth, resilience, and strategic planning. Picture the legacy you can craft, one where financial fear doesn't define you but guide you towards better decisions.

Everyone has different starting points and goals when it comes to investing. Maybe you're a young professional like Sarah, taking those first confident strides into the stock market. Or perhaps you're someone who prefers the steadiness of bonds or the diversified safety of mutual funds. Each path is valid. The key is understanding your options and making informed choices that align with your timeline and risk tolerance.

Financial literacy is a lifelong journey, much like learning a new language. Think about it - initially, simple phrases help you get by, but as you delve deeper, you start grasping complex nuances. You might face setbacks, but the trick is to keep learning and stay informed.

Let's simplify a crucial concept - keeping your emotions in check. The market will fluctuate; it's as predictable as the tide. Experienced investors understand this and stay the course. New investors often struggle, feeling anxious with every dip.

Financial planning also involves understanding the broader economic forces at play. For instance, inflation—sometimes referred to as the "silent wealth eroder"—can affect your purchasing power over time. Keeping an eye on economic indicators and adjusting your strategy ensures that your savings don't lose value. This vigilance plays a critical role in maintaining financial health.

You've learned about the tools - budgeting, saving, stocks, bonds, mutual funds, and diversification. Now it's about integrating these tools into a cohesive strategy. Let's carry forward the knowledge that building wealth isn't a sprint; it's a marathon requiring persistence, patience, and planning. Visualize your goals, track your progress, and adjust as needed. Just like in any endeavor, consistency and informed decision-making are the compasses that steer you toward financial success.

You have what it takes to build a thriving financial legacy. Here's to your journey, and may it be as rewarding and enriching as you envision.

References

This book draws upon a wide range of sources that provide insights, data, and strategies related to personal finance.

Books

- **Dave Ramsey** - *The Total Money Makeover: A Proven Plan for Financial Fitness* (2003): A comprehensive guide to budgeting, saving, and debt management.

- **Robert Kiyosaki** - *Rich Dad Poor Dad* (1997): Insights into financial independence and the mindset necessary for building wealth.

- **Benjamin Graham** - *The Intelligent Investor* (1949): A foundational text on value investing, focusing on long-term strategies and managing risk.

- **Ramit Sethi** - *I Will Teach You to Be Rich* (2009): A practical guide to budgeting, saving, and investing, with an emphasis on automation.

- **John C. Bogle** - *The Little Book of Common Sense Investing* (2007): Advocacy for low-cost index funds as a long-term investment strategy.

Websites

- **Investopedia** - *Investing and Financial Education Resource*. Available at: https://www.investopedia.com

- **NerdWallet** - *Personal Finance and Budgeting Tools*. Available at: https://www.nerdwallet.com

- **The Balance** - *Comprehensive Financial Guides*. Available at: https://www.thebalance.com

- **Morningstar** - *Investment Research and Analysis*. Available at: https://www.morningstar.com

Magazines & Journals

- **Forbes Magazine** - *Money & Investing Section* (April 2024): Articles on current trends in personal finance and investing strategies.

- **Money Magazine** - *Budgeting & Savings Special Issue* (June 2024): Practical tips and strategies for managing personal finances effectively.

- **The Wall Street Journal** - *Personal Finance Section* (July 2024): Regular coverage of financial planning, market insights, and investment strategies.

- **Kiplinger's Personal Finance** - *Annual Investing Guide* (May 2024): Detailed guidance on investing, retirement planning, and wealth management.

Further Reading

To deepen your understanding of financial literacy, consider exploring the following books and resources:

- **Elizabeth Warren & Amelia Warren Tyagi** - *All Your Worth: The Ultimate Lifetime Money Plan* (2005): A practical guide to managing finances and achieving balance in spending.

- **Tony Robbins** - *Unshakeable: Your Financial Freedom Playbook* (2017): Focuses on building a strong, diversified portfolio for financial security.

- **Suze Orman** - *The Money Book for the Young, Fabulous & Broke* (2005): Tailored advice for younger individuals starting their financial journey.

- **Morgan Housel** - *The Psychology of Money: Timeless Lessons on Wealth, Greed, and Happiness* (2020): Explores how behavior and mindset impact financial success.

- **Andrew Hallam** - *Millionaire Teacher: The Nine Rules of Wealth You Should Have Learned in School* (2011): A guide to wealth-building through simple, disciplined investing strategies.

- **Carl Richards** - *The Behavior Gap: Simple Ways to Stop Doing Dumb Things with Money* (2012): Discusses common financial mistakes and how to avoid them.

- **Jean Chatzky** - *Make Money, Not Excuses* (2008): Empowers women to take control of their finances with practical tips and strategies.

Resources

For ongoing learning and practical tools, the following online resources can be extremely helpful:

- Investopedia: A comprehensive resource for investing education, market analysis, and financial terms.

- NerdWallet: Offers tools and advice on budgeting, credit cards, loans, and investing.

- **The Balance**: Provides in-depth guides on personal finance topics including saving, investing, and retirement planning.

- **Mint.com**: A free online service for tracking your spending, creating budgets, and managing finances.

- **YNAB (You Need A Budget)**: A budgeting tool that helps you gain control of your money and achieve financial goals.

- **Morningstar**: A resource for researching and analyzing investments, particularly mutual funds and ETFs.

- **Bogleheads**: A community forum dedicated to discussions on investing and personal finance, based on the principles of John C. Bogle.